The Tribulation Hand-Book

FOR THOSE LEFT BEHIND WHEN JESUS CHRIST
COMES FOR HIS CHURCH OF BELIEVERS

Albert J. Lynch

Order this book online at www.trafford.com
or email orders@trafford.com

Most Trafford titles are also available at major online book retailers.

Printed in the United States of America.

ISBN: 978-1-4669-8826-2 (sc)
ISBN: 978-1-4669-8825-5 (e)

Trafford rev. 08/21/2013

 www.trafford.com

North America & international
toll-free: 1 888 232 4444 (USA & Canada)
fax: 812 355 4082

INDEX OF CHAPTERS TO THE TRIBULATION HAND-BOOK

ABOUT THE BOOK

This Book is aimed at the people who will occupy the earth; after people like me are raptured out of the earth; into the presence of the Living God, Jesus Christ.

You have left here with the antichrist and his false prophet; and the devil, who was kicked out of second heaven at the time we went up to meet our maker.

Also the Holy Spirit was taken of the earth with us; that leaves at the mercy of the antichrist, who is raised back from the dead; after being shot in the head. You will be forced to worship a image of the antichrist or die. Who wants to worship a cartoon.

There is still time; while you are physically alive to accept the Lord Jesus Christ as your Savior (from your sins) and as your Lord God.

You must understand that you are a sinner; and need the forgiveness of God. In order to have a relationship with Him.

In a way, you have more physical evidence that there is a God; than the people that have been taken off the earth.

You have seen Him come for His Church of Believers at the rapture of the Church of Believers. You have seen Him. You know He is real; thats more than the people that have been taken off the earth had; they had to believe in Him by Faith; but faith in God is what you did not have; thats why you were left were you are.

The reason you did not have any faith in God is that you have pride in the false religion that you could not be moved from by the people that have preached Jesus Christ to you.

Read on.

Now you must believe in The Lord Jesus Christ with your whole being; because you are going to have to die for him; better to die for Jesus Christ than to live for the devil.

This whole Book is a learning experience. The Lord, Jesus Christ showed us when He wanted to come in September 16/17, 2012. He did not come at that time. He delayeth his coming; that's in Matthew 24:48. We know that the time of His coming is in the Bible.

We are now in the Minor Tribulation; that started January 1, 2013.

2012 to 2022 are the years that finish The Bible; and we the people who are raptured along with you; the people who are left behind on the earth; will either be in Heaven or condemned to the lake of fire by 2022. There is no future for anybody on this earth after 2022.

Author's Note: This Book is intentionally kept short. The spacing on the printing is double spaced; so that it can be read in low light conditions. When you read this; I will be gone!

ABOUT THE AUTHOR

I am the author of "The Message". The previously published Book that shows the acceptable time of the end of our world in the Bible as put there by my God and your God to warn us the people who inhabit the earth at this time to be aware of the serious events that will soon take place.

After having "The Message published in August 2012; I was very concerned about getting the information of the "Message" into the hands of the reader; because the "Message" called for The Rapture to be on September 16/17th 2012.

It didn't happen on the day it was suppose to happen. The day was not cloudy; as it talks about in Ezekiel 30:3

#) "For the day is near, even the day of the Lord is near, a Cloudy day; it shall be the time of the heathen."

The time of the heathen; is a clue that it will be in the future. This prompted me to read on and I found in Matthew 24:48

#48) "But and if that evil servant shall say in his heart, my Lord delayeth his coming.

So The Lord God delayeth His Coming; because he is the giver of all things that are good; and he is waiting for an earthly event to take place; so that He can rescue His Church of Believers from the antichrist in the lesser Tribulation period.

Yes, I said Tribulation period. 2013 corresponds to chapter 13 in the Book Of Revelation. The antichrist and his prophet are introduced to the reader; ending with his 666 number of identification.

Chapter 12 in the Book of Revelation pertains to the year 2012

Before we get into 2012 in the Book of Revelation. Here is another verse that I have found pertaining to the time of the end.

Habakkuk 2:2. verse 2:2 "For the vision is yet for an appointed time, But at the end; it shall speak, and not lie; though it tarry, wait for it, because it will surely come, it will not tarry."

This is another verse to show that the rapture of the Church of Believers was delayed; because of the events on the earth to take place; and all the Bible prophecys to be fullfilled.

Back to 2012; In the Book of revelation, the twelveth chapter and the nineth verse it says: verse 12:9 "And the great dragon was castout, that old serpent, called the devil, and satan, which decieveth the whole world: He was cast out into the earth, and his angels were cast out with him."

This verse ties in with September 2012 in the accepted time of the Rapture of the Church of Believers.

Isaiah 61:2: "and Luke 4:19 both say the same thing. Here is Isaiah 61:2 "To proclaim the acceptable year of the Lord, and the day of vengeance of our God; to comfort all that mourn."

Luke 4:19 "To preach the acceptable year of The Lord." 2012 was the acceptable year of the Lord!

On the next page is a handbil that I personally put on cars in Church Parking lots starting two Sundays before the 16th of September 2012. At that Time I was convinced that some how the right date for the end of the world was the night of the 16? 17 night of September 2012.

I did not use or intend to sell copies of the "Message". My thought was to offer it for a reference to interested People.

After the Handbill on the next page is a copy of a page that was left out of the original publication of the "Message".

You and your family are invited to a Big Party

on Sunday September 16/17th at midnight this year 2012

It's The Rapture of The Church of Christian Believers.

The place: Where you are standing at midnight will be just fine. What you must bring to the party or you will not be allowed to enter.

In order to be admitted to the party: where you will meet people you have not seen, since they died believing in The Lord, Jesus Christ as their Lord and Savior. You and I must also believe in the Lord Jesus Christ as Our Lord and Savior to gain admission.

You must believe in your heart, that The Lord Jesus Christ was sent by The Father God, to be the offering before God for the remission of all sin; by shedding His Blood, so that the people on the earth can one day see God in The person of Jesus Christ.

Without this one requirement; you will not be admitted to the Rapture of the Church of Believers.

This is what will happen on that night: 1 Thessalonians 4:16 and 17. Notice how the verse numbers match the calendar dates.

16) "For the Lord Himself shall descend from heaven with a shout, and the voice of the archangel, and the trump of God: and the dead shall rise first".

17) "Then we which are alive and remain shall be caught up together with them in the clouds, to meet the Lord in the air; and so shall ever be with The Lord".

What Jesus will Shout: Hebrews 10:9. "Then said He, Lo, I come to do thy will, O God. He taketh away the first, that He may establish the second". Note: The Christian Believers are first to leave the earth; and the Jews who did not accept Jesus Christ when He came on earth; with other non believers remain on the earth; with the Devil who is thrown out of second heaven to earth; to go into a seven year tribulation period; known as the 70th week of Daniel.

After this seven year period; the saved people of the earth are treated to a thousand years of living on the reconstructed earth.

If you are interested in this party get the Book called, "The Message". Trafford Publishing, amazon.com.

The Lord Jesus Christ did not come for His church of Believes on that 16-17 of September 2012. I believe that was the date that He wanted to come; using all the Holidays from Exodus Chapter 20. But He has given us more time; and given the Church into the minor Tribulation Period; which has started on January 1, 2013.

Evil has grown in this year and people are accepting Gay Marriage as a normal way of life.

The people that are involved in practicing this from of social conduct; are not in Love; but Bondage.

Bondage is when the person commits sin; they have given their life over to the devil and he just makes them want to commit more of the same kind of sin. This is being mistaking for human love. It takes a strong about face to brake this hold of the devil on the person involved.

A sincere act of contrition; asking God for forgiveness and not committing the sin anymore; would be the answer to the curse of the devil.

CHAPTER 1

"Why am I still Here"

I will assume that the reader of this writing; is reading this after the 17th of September 2012.

You and all the others who are still on the earth saw The Lord, Jesus Christ, come for His church of Believers.

The last book of the Bible, the Book of revelation has God's description of that event in Rev. 1:7.

"Behold, He cometh with clouds and every eye shall see Him. And they also which pierced Him: and all kindreds of the earth shall wail because of Him. Even so. Amen".

Half of the people on the earth were taken; the other half to remain on earth for the Tribulation period of seven years.

From The Book of Matthew 24:40. "Then shall two be in the field The one shall be taken, and other left." Matthew 24:41. "Two women shall be grinding, at the mill. One shall be taken, and the other left."

The one who witnessed this event and recorded it for you to hear now is no other than Jesus Christ Himself.

The people that are gone are the Believers in Jesus Christ as their Savior. And also believe in the holy Trinity of God, The Father, and The Son, and The Holy Ghost.

The reason that you and the other half of the population of the earth at this time are still here is that you and the others HAVE NOT MADE A PERSONAL RELATIONSHIP WITH The Lord and Savior Jesus Christ.

Did you have a relationship with the Lord Jesus Christ and gave it up for something to met your worldly needs?

Any other belief with no Jesus Christ as The Savior will get you confinded to the earth at this time period.

Our God wants all men to saved; but He will not force you to do anything not of your own free will. He created you. He knows your thoughts.

He wants you to see that you need Him; not only to escape YOUR SITUATION OF NOW WITH THE DEVIL IN THE PERSON IN reincarnated with the body of King Juan Carlos of Spain.

Here is what Jesus Christ says to the last of the seven Churches.

Rev. 3:14 thru 22

14) And unto the—ANGEL of the church of Laodica write: these things saith The Amen, The Faithful and true Witness, the beginning of the creation of God.

15) I know thy works, that thou ARE NEITHER COLD NOR HOT. I would thu wert cold or hot.

16) So then because thou art lukewarm, and neither cold or hot, I will spue thee out of my mouth.

17) Because thou sayest, I am rich, and increased with goods, and have need of nothing; and knowest not that thou art wretched and miserable, and poor, and blind, and naked.

18) I consel thee to buy of me gold tried in fire, that THOU MAYEST be rich; and white raiment, that thou mayest be clothed, and that shame of thy nakedness do not appear; and anoint thine eyes with eye-eye-salve, that thou mayest see.

19) As many as I love, I rebuke and chasten. Be zealous therefore, and repent.

20) Behold I stand at the door and knock: If any man hear my voice, and open the door, I will come in to him, and will sup with him, and he with me.

21) To Him that overcometh; will I grant to sit with me in my throne, even a as I overcame, anam set down with My Father in His throne.

22) He that hath an ear, let him hear what the spirit saith unto the Churches.

Wow! The Holy Spirit has been taken out of this world and and He left a message for you personally.

This is your invitation to be in the same place as the people that were taken from the earth in the night of September 17th, 2012.

Whatever you believe at this time is not sufficient to get you in the presence of God. You should now be able to see that you place in time is serious and; your belief, whatever it is needs to be changed so that you may have a relation ship with almighty God.

We the Believers, believe in The Divine Trinity. As you can see; Jesus Christ, Himself, offers an invitation to you; who He left behind to now come to Him. An offer to overcome your position as one who has been left after the rapture of The Church of Believers, on September 17th 2012.

In verse 21 and verse 22, He speaks of the oneness with the Father and all with The Holy Spirit.

You the reader has been preached to concerning the accepting of Jesus Christ as your personal Savior and Master and God. What? you turned Jesus Christ down?

Mark 16:15. "And He said unto them. Go ye into all the world and preach the Gospel to every creature.

It is never to late as long as your still physically alive.

You are in this tribulation period because you turned down Jesus Christ when it was presented to accept Him as your Lord and Savior. You turned down your invitation to Salvation. You can still make up for your loss by now being sorry for your sins, and accepting Jesus Christ as your lord and Savior.

The time that you are now in; demands that you are convinced that the decision that you have made is a final decision and have the courage as a martyr for your cause.

If you are asked to take the mark of the beast. You must refuse; and accept the consequences.

This will put you on the road to Salvation and eternal life.

The next page will show you, the Roman Road to Salvation.

Our God is a Jew, and if you were adopted into a Jewish household; you would get no inheritance; but if you were adopted in a Roman House-hold you would get full inheritance. The same as your adopted brothers or sisters; that is why God had the salvation verses put in the Book of Romans.

You cannot give your allegiance to the devil in this life; for he has no future; and you would be lost as he is going to be for sure as I write these words to you; and you are now reading them.

Look now on the next page and follow the Roman road as many before you have.

If you want to be saved; you must take a walk through the Book of Romans in the Bible.

Why the Book of Romans?

When you are saved; you are adopted in the family of God.

Jesus Christ was and is a Jew; if you were adopted into a Jewish household; you receive no inheritance. This is why Our God had the verses necessary for salvation put in the Book of Romans. If you were adopted into a Roman household; you would receive full inheritance as the naturally others who were born into the household.

The Roman Walk

1)   Romans 3:10: "As it is written, there is none righteous, no, not one".

2)   Romans 3:23 "For all have sinned, and come short of the Glory of God".

3)   Romans 5:12: "Wherefore, as by one man sin entered into the world and death by sin; and so death passed upon all men, for that all have sinned;

4)   Romans 6:23: "For the wages of sin is death; but The Gift of God is eternal life; though Jesus Christ, Our Lord".

5)   Romans 5:8: "But God commendeth His love toward us, in that while we were yet sinners, Christ died for us".

6)   Romans 10:13 "For whosoever shall call upon the name of the Lord; shall be saved."

7)   Romans 10:9 and 10:

9) "That if thou confess with thy mouth The Lord Jesus, and shall believe in thine heart that God hath raised Him from the dead, thou shalt be saved". 10) For with the heart man believeth into righteous; and with the mouth confession is made unto Salvation."

The seventh week of Daniel

Roman empire, the antichrist and his false prophet to find the last of the christian Believers; who before the rapture of the Church of Christian Believers would not give up their pride in the false religion that they believed in.

Our president Obama, really finished off from the blessings of God; when he said, "I think gays should get Married".

Now in 2013 or chapter thirteen of the Book of Revelation; we have a this time a new Pope being elected in late March 2013. He will be the false prophet for the antichrist, King Juan Carlos of Spain.

The antichrist and his prophet, the new Pope will have the full reign of the planet earth; after the Christian Believers, and the Holy spirit are removed from the earth at the rapture; which you the reader has missed. They will incorporate a system of Identification the same as they are now using on dogs and cats to establish their identity for their owners.

A very small micro-chip is injected by a needle in the forehead or the top of the right hand and can be read with a wand attached to a computer to read out the information, about the person.

Anyone who willing accepts this mark of the beast will for sure lose all hope of ever being saved from the lake of fire; where the antichrist, the devil; and the false prophet will be thrown into.

Your only hope; if you are asked to take the mark of the beast is to reject it and accept the consequences; which is death.

This is your only path to salvation; unless you can evade the antichrist for seven years. He most likely will employ all Nations their armies their police forces to accomplish he wishes.

The antichrist is a high degree mason; and he has many brothers around the world.

Daniel (:21 thru 27

21) "Yea, whiles I was speaking in prayer, even the man Gabriel, whom I had seen in the vision at the beginning, being caused to fly swiftly, touched me about the time of the evening oblation.

22) "And He informed me, and talked with me, and said, O Daniel, I am come forth to give thee skill and understanding"

23) "At the beginning of thy supplications the commandment came forth, for thou art greatly beloved: therefore understand the matter, and consider the vision."

24) "Seventy weeks are determined upon thy people and upon the holy city, to finish the transgression, to make reconciliation for iniquity, and to bring in everlasting righteousness, and seal up the vision and prophecy, and to anoint the Most Holy."

25) "Know therefore and understand, that from the going forth of the commandment to restore and to build Jerusalem unto the Messiah the

prince shall be seven weeks, and threescore and two weeks: The street shall be built again, and the wall, even in troublous times".

26) "And after threescore and two weeks shall the Messiah be cut off, but not of Himself: and the people of the prince that shall come shall destroy the city and the sanctuary; and the end thereof shall be with a flood, and unto the end of the war desolations are determined".

27) "And he shall confirm the covenant with many one week: and in the midst of the week he will cause the sacrifice and the oblation to cease, and for the overspreading of Abominations he shall make it desolate, even until the consummation, and that determined shall be poured upon the desolate,"

As told to the prophet Daniel: this is God's plan to use the Roman Empire, the antichrist, King Juan Carlos

CHAPTER 2
"Strength of Seeing Him"

There is a story of which I think is pertenate to your situation. The story of Saint Thomas. One of the original twelve Apostles.

Our story begins in John 20:24.

But Thomas, one of the twelve, called Didymus was not with them WHEN JESUS CAME, 25) THE OTHER DISCIPLES SAID UNTO HIM, WE HAVE SEEN THE THE LORD. BUT HE SAID THEM. EXCEPT I SEE IN HIS HANDS, THE PRINT OF THE nails, and put my finger into the print of the nails, and thrust my hand into His side, I will not believe.

26) And after eight days again His disciples were with in, and Thomas with them. Then came Jesus, the doors were shut, and stood in their midst, and said peace be with you.

27) Then saith He to Thomas, reach hither thy finger, and behold my hands, reach hither thy hand and thrust it into my side.; and be not faithless, but believing.

28) And Thomas answered and said unto Him. My Lord and My God.

29) Jesus saith unto him, Thomas, because THOU hast seen Me, thou hast believed: Blessed are they that have not seen, and yet believed.

30) And many other signs truly did Jesus in the presence of his disciples, which are not written in this book.

31) But these are written, that ye might believe that Jesus is the Christ, The Son of God, and that believing ye might have life though His name.

You the reader have had the same experience as Thomas. You have seen The Lord Jesus Christ. When He came for His Church of Believers.

That Church of Believers was called The Philadelphia Church the Church of brotherly love. You are in the last Church, the seventh Church. The Church of Laodicea.

The next chapters will pertain to the Book of Revelation; which is synonymous with the time period you are in.

The earlier chapters describes the people who have been removed from the earth as believers, for the last 6 thousand years.

A discretion of God's throne and how important the churches are to Him. The judgements that will come upon the earth to try the people of the earth.

Chapters 12 thru 22 give an highlight to each of the seven years of the Tribulation period you are in.

CHAPTER 3

"The Strength of Seeing Jesus Christ"

At the Rapture of The Church of Believers; The writer or The Book of Revelation, John writes; Chapter 1:7,: Behold, He cometh with clouds and every eye shall see Him, and they also which pieced Him, and all kindreds of the earth shall wail because of Him."

You if you are reading this published Book; called The Tribulation Hand-Book". In the year 2013; you are one of the people; that were left behind. I reiterate this because of it's importance.

The Church of the people that have been taken away by The Lord, Jesus Christ were never given the gift of seeing Him; they had to believe in Him by Faith.

This is all in God's Plan to give you the Knowledge by seeing Him come for His Believers. You have an earthly knowledge by sight, to confirm to your non-believing heart that Our God is a real person; who cares about His people; who love Him.

This is all in God's plan; He knows the Future, the past and the present. This added gift of sight of His coming for His Believers was to let you know where you are left behind.

He knows ahead of time; who will be saved; and who will be lost.

You are not lost yet. You must deny the Devil and his works. Even if it means your life here on earth; but what kind of life is it on earth with the Devil in the person of the antichrist, King Juan Carlos of Spain; to be the ruler over all the peoples of the earth for the seven Year Tribulation Period.

If you have any kind of morals; (belief in right and wrong) with the prospect of going to hell with the antichrist and His prophet, The Pope of the catholic church; who the antichrist kills during the seven year period; so that He can say he is God.

This Rapture event will happen on July 7, 2013 at the midnight. The information comes from Ezechiel, Chapter 7 and verse 7; the whole chapter should be read. It will be printed later on.

Please note:

I, The Author, Albert J. Lynch would not have known that Chapters, 12 thru 22 of the Book of Revelation pertain to the years; if I had not written the Book called "THE MESSAGE".

The key to this knowledge is found in Chapter 12, verse 9. "The Great dragon was cast out, that old serpent, called the devil, in the Book of Revelation. The last Book of the Bible.

2012 The year relates to Chapter 12. The year 2012 is a *leap year*.
The Rapture of The Church of Believers takes place.
The devil is thrown out of Heaven; becomes the Antichrist

The start of the seven year Tribulation period on earth.

2013 The year relates to Chapter 13.

2014 The year relates to Chapter 14.

2015 The year relates to Chapter 15.

2016 The year relates to Chapter 16. A *leap year*.
The center of the seven year Tribulation period falls in this year.

The Antichrist does the Abomination of Desolation in the New temple in Jerusalem.

2017 The year relates to Chapter 17.

2018 The year relates to Chapter 18.

2019 The year relates to Chapter 19.

2020 The year relates to Chapter 20. A *leap year*.

The end of the seven year tribulation period.

2021 The year relates to Chapter 21.

2022 The year relates to Chapter 22. ETERNITY STARTS

3 ½ Years

3 ½ Years

Seven Year Tribulation Period

A final invite from The Lord Jesus Christ to whomever will listen to Him, 1000 years for the Christian Believers to live on a new earth in their human Bodies,; Then the final judgement of the dead. The ones that did not accept Jesus Christ as their Savior. Then comes eternity, no more time.

CHAPTER 4

"Good Deeds"

Sorry, you cannot get to Heaven by doing what you call good deeds. You cannot attain rightness with Our God.

Isaiah 64:6 "But we are all as unclean thing, and our righteousnesses, are as filthy rags; and all we do fad as a leaf; and all our iniquities like the wind, have taken us away."

Some other quotes that would interest you are:

2 Corinthians 11:14 "And no marvel, for Satan himself is transformed into an angel of light."

Matthew 23:4 to 12

4)   For they bind heavy burdens and grievous to be borne, and lay them on men's shoulders; but they themselves will not move them with one of their fingers."

5)   But all their works they do for to be seen of men: they make broad their phylacteries, and enlarge the borders of their garments".

6)   "And love the uppermost rooms feasts, and the chief seats in the synagogues."

7)   "And greetings in the markets and to be called of men, Rabbi, Rabbi."

8)   "But be not ye called Rabbi: for one is your Master, even Christ, and all ye are brethern."

9)   And call no man your Father upon the earth: for One is your Father, which is in heaven."

10) Neither be ye called Master; for One is your Master, even Christ."

11) But he that is greatest among you shall be your servant."

12) "And whomever shall exalt himself shall be abased; and he that shall humble himself shall be exalted."

Did you get out of the above quotes; the meaning of what is said?

No Good Deeds, no good works, Do not call any one on earth your Father. Do not be called Master or call any one on the earth Master.

You cannot do good deeds to make a relationship with our God. You cannot call no man your Father on earth; This knocks out the catholic church; Also do not call any man your Master on Earth. That knocks out the Masons; and all others that have a man at the head of the religion.

CHAPTER 5

"The Supreme Being"

Remember that when ever I can; I will use Bible Quotes to prove my point. They are the true God's Word and every time you read them Faith is acquired by you. Romans 10:17. "So then Faith cometh by hearing, and hearing by The Word of God."

Revelation 20 verses 1 and 2 "And I saw an angel come down from Heaven having the key to the bottomless pit; and a great chain in his hand'.

2)   "And he laid hold of the dragon, that old serpent, which is the Devil, and Satan, and bound him a thousand years.'"

John 10:19. "The thief cometh not, but for to steal, and to Kill, and to destroy; But I am come that they might have life, and that they might have it more abundantly."

2 Corinthians 11:14 "And no marvel, for Satan Himself is transformed into an angel of light".

Revelation 12:9, 10

9)   "and the great dragon was cast out, that old serpent, called the Devil,

      and Satan, which decieveth the whole world: he was cast out into the

      earth, and his angels were cast out with him."

10)   and I heard a loud voice saying in Heaven, now is come salvation, and

      strength, and the Kingdom of our God, and the power of Christ: for

      the accuser of the brethern is casy down, which accused them before

      God, day and night."

This one "supreme being" to some. The Devil is transformed into an angel
of light. Where does he get that light from; if he is the epitome of darkness?.

As he stands in second Heaven with Jesus Christ accusing the brethren, he
is standing in the presence of God the Father; which is in first Heaven; and the
light for the Father shines through the Devil, the accuser.

When the Devil is thrown out of second Heaven; he will no longer be in
The presence of God The Father; he will shine no more.

The throwing out of second Heaven does occur at the rapture of The church of
Believers on The Seventh of July 2013 at midnight. The devil is now with you on
earth; in the person of King Juan Carlos of Spain. He will receive a shot in the head
an appear to be dead; but the Devil will reincarnate back to life.

King Juan Carlos is an accomplish student of military strategy, and tactics.
He will defend Isreal against the Russians.

CHAPTER 6

"Baptism"

The Four Baptisms; The Baptism of water, The Baptism of The Spirit: The Baptism of Desire, and the Baptism of Blood.

Baptism of water is what a convert to Christianity; voluntarily receives to establish a closer relationship with Jesus Christ.

The process involves the individual seeing a need for forgiveness from his or her sins; and accepting Jesus Christ as their Savior from sin. This water Baptism leads to for some; the second Baptism, which is The Baptism of The Spirit. This Baptism is administered by a Bible believing Minister by the laying on of hands. The Holy Spirit is invited in; to get a knowledge from God; concerning what He wants you to know about him; as He reveals Himself while reading His Bible.

The Baptism of Desire is for someone who knows that water Baptism is impossible. A dying man in a hospital, some one that knows they are about to die and does not want to go to the grave without telling Jesus Christ how much they need Him as their Savior and Their Lord and Master.

The Baptism of Blood is the last Baptism and most assuredly the most dramatic event of a person's life. This Baptism is for those people who in times past; were Martyred for what they believed in; But this is true in your Seven Year Tribulation period.

You must put your trust in God as the people before you did. If you are truly a man, you should be willing to die for what you believe in; but if you cannot believe you will take the mark of the beast 666 and accompany the Devil to hell. Once you take the mark of the beast in your right hand or forehead. You are lost to eternity.

In your situation with the antichrists military and police looking for those who will not take the mark of the beast. It seems more likely than not you will be hunted down and put to the test of weither you will accept the mark of the beast; and you know now, it means eternal damnation. In Hell with the Devil for eternity.

What would you do? I know what I would do. I would accept Jesus Christ and refuse to take the mark of the beast.

If that means the end of my natural life than so be it.

This earth is only a test for you and me. I passed my test; I am already in Heaven with my Lord Jesus Christ; but you are still being tested on earth. Although you have seen The Lord when He came for His Believers the night of July 18, 2013. The Lord's delayed coming. The rapture of The Church of Christian Believers.

CHAPTER 7

"Who is our God"

If we read the first Book of the Bible; you will see the time period you are in. The period you are in is the third time Our God has tryed to obtain a people on earth, that was worthy of having a relationship with Him in Heaven.

The first time was in Chapter 1 verse 2. We read. "And the earth was with out form, and void, and darkness was upon the face of the deep. And the Spirit of God moved upon the waters."

Note: The earth was covered by water. He had destroyed the previous generations of His creations of people because they were not living in a manner that was acceptable to Him.

Death by drowning.

This fact is proven in Genesis 1:28 (Adam and Eve's world)

(The second try). "And Blessed them and said unto them; be fruitful and multiply and replenish the earth.

Replenish means to resupply with. In this case; resupply people!

That was the first time as we know that God Destroyed the World and the people in it.

Then after the flood of Adam's world. The second time He used the flood to destroy the world. God says to Noah and His three sons. In Genesis 9:1. "And God blessed Noah and his sons, and said unto them be fruitful and multiply, and replenish the earth".

The period of time you are in; is the third try by our God to get a people acceptable to having a long relationship with Him.

Three stricks and you are out! That would not work here. Although you must realize that Our God could not come back again and offer himself on the cross for another group of people living in a next try at finding people suitable for God.

Man has but one life, death and the judgement; that is His own rule. No there is no reincarnation.

There is no trying after you come of the earth. Either you will be saved and go with God through Eternity; or you will be condemned to be with Satan, the Devil in Hell for Eternity. The choice is up to you.

Did you ever see a rainbow in the sky after it rained? Guess who put it there? Genesis Chapter 9:11. "And I will establish my covenant with you, neither shall all flesh be cut off any more by the waters of a flood; neither shall there any more be a flood to destroy the earth.

12) And God said, This is the token of the covenant which I make between me and you and every living creature that is with you, for perpetual generations.

13) I do set my bow in the cloud, and it shall be for a token of a covenant between Me and the earth."

14) And it shall come to pass, when I bring a cloud over the earth, that the bow shall be seen in the cloud."

15) And I will remember my covenant, which is between Me and you and every living creature of all flesh; and the waters shall no more become a flood to destroy all flesh."

16) And the bow shall be in the cloud; and I will look upon it, that I may remember the ever lasting covenant between God and every Living creature of all flesh that is upon the earth."

Every time you see a rainbow; you will know that God is looking at it too. Although, I do not know if there be any rainbows in Tribulation.

John 3:16. "For God so loved the world, that He gave His only begotten Son, that whosoever believeth in Him shall not perish, but have everlasting life."

In order to pay for all the sins of the world The Father God gave His only Son to be sacrificed for the remission of all sin. John 3:16. "For God so loved the world, that He gave His only begotten Son, that whosoever believeth in Him should not perish, but have everlasting life."

John 17. "For God sent not His Son into the world to condemn the world; but that the world through Him might be saved."

18. "He that believeth on Him is not condemned: but he that believeth not not is condemned already, because he hath not believed in the name of the only begotten Son of God."

19. "And this is the condemnation, that light is come into the world, and men loved darkness rather than light, because their deeds were evil."

20. "For every one that doeth evil, hateth the light, neither cometh to the light, lest his deeds should be reproved".

21. "But he that doeth truth cometh to the light, that his deeds may be made manifest, that they are wrought of God."

John 4:24. "God is a spirit: and they that worship Him must worship Him in Spirit. "and in truth".

CHAPTER 8

"The Church of Laodicea"

The members of this group of people who remain on the earth; after the Rapture of The Church of Christian Believers; are known by our God Jesus Christ as those who lack the necessary amount of Faith needed to make the requirement for Salvation.

If you are reading this in a Book authored by me. Then you are among those described above.

Revelation 4:15 & 16:

"15) I know thy works, that thou art neither cold nor hot, I would thou wert cold or hot."

"16) So then because thou art lukewarm, and neither cold nor hot: I will spue thee out of my mouth."

Comment: Verse 15, describes a person who knows what is what Our God desires of us; but is too busy living the easy life or should I say the earthly life to give their lives to Jesus Christ.

Comment: Verse 16, Jesus Christ tells of the fate of those who are lukewarm. "I will spue thee out of my Mouth", means that His protection is taken away; and the person in question joins the others; who are left behind. Left behind now with the devil in the body of the antichrist, King Juan Carlos, of Spain.

In order to be Saved and enjoy the same situation as those who have been previously Taken up to be with Our God; you must build you Faith in God.

Romans 10:17: "So then Faith cometh by hearing, and hearing by the word of God." So get yourself a Bible, King James 1611; or any Bible, and read the Books of the New Testament; out loud to yourself, or anybody that feels like you do. This is the only way; you can increase your Faith in God at this time.

You can start by walking down the Roman Rood as many people have done on their rood to Salvation. It follows on the next page of this Book.

There is no other planet with people on it; only the earth with it's large number of people; and you are one of them.

Our God has instituted the Blood attonement for Sin; when He killed those two animals in the Garden of Eden, for Adam and Eve. Jesus Christ The Son of God was used by God The Father to be the offering, The high Priest, and The Sacrifice of His Blood for the remission of all sin of the people of the world.

It must be explained here that we are talking about a three person entity; The Holy Trinity. Father God, one person; The Son, Jesus Christ; and The Holy Ghost, the Third person of the Holy Trinity. It is the same way with us, Body, soul, and spirit.

God The Father modeled human beings after himself. The proof is in Genesis Chapter 1:26. "And God said, Let us make man in our image, after our likeness.

Notice the plurals used in the sentence. Let us, our, and our. So it should not be to hard for anyone to accept God as He is.

But what that means is that if Jesus Christ, The son of God; went to die on the cross; then The Father was present in Him also; as was The Holy Ghost the Third person of the Holy Trinity.

Jesus Christ is the human member of The Holy Trinity; that we are common with in having but one life here on earth death, and the judgement.

Hebrews 9:27, "And it is appointed unto men once to die, but after this the judgement." Our Lord and Savior Jesus Christ, who is God almighty had to abide by His own law. He was born as all men are born into the world thru a woman; and lived and was crucified in death for the sins of the world. note; The term "men or Man" is used here to denote the basic creation of God. Man is the person who is unsaved. After he or she decides to accept Jesus Christ as Lord and Savior; God look upon them as as a Son or Daughter of His; but that situation was only present before the Rapture of the Church of Believers.

At this time, in the Seven Year Tribulation Period; God has no relationship with the people that were left behind, no protection from the devil who is on earth looking for people to spoil their salvation and go with him and his prophet the Pope to Hell for eternity.

Yet the hand of God does reach into the tribulation period to save some people. As you will see in further reading. Could you be one of them?

The last book of the Bible, The Book of Revelation has twenty two chapters. The first 11 chapters describes The seven Churches, God's throne Room, and some of the pain and suffering that people that have turned their back on God; and have walked after other Gods.

Chapters 12 thru 22 describe the years of the seven year tribulation period that we are now in. February 22, 2013 is the date as I write this. 2013. Chapter 13 or the year 2013 is the first year of the start of Seven years of Tribulation. The first 3½ years are called The Minor Tribulation. Then we have the center of Tribulation with the Abomination-of Desolation taking place in the new temple by the antichrist saying he is God. The next 3½ years is called the Great Tribulation. This is God's way of punishing the people who have taken the mark of the beast, 666 on their right hand or on their forehead.

But let us first start with Chapter twelve or the year 2012.

The year 2012 as described in the Bible book of revelation with Isreal fighting with other nations over the land of Isreal.

In verse 9 of chapter twelve; that translate to the year 2012 and the month of September. "And the great dragon was cast out, that old serpent, called the devil, and satan, which decieveth the whole world was cast out, into the earth, and his angels were cast out with him."

The casting out of the devil out of second heaven to earth is in line with God's acceptable year of the end of time. The chapter and verse are in line with "The Message"; which was previously published by this same company: proving God wanted to end this world on September 16/17 2012; but he delayed His coming for His Church of Believers; probably to give more time to the people who need to change their lives around from bad to good; so that they can join the rest of The Church of Believers; and be ready when He comes.

The year of 2012 was the Acceptable year of the coming of The Lord as published in "The Message".

Isaiah 61:2 "To proclaim the acceptable year of The Lord, and the vengeance of our God, to comfort all that moun".

Luke 4:18 & 19

18) "The spirit of The Lord is upon me, because he hath anointed me to preach the Gospel to the poor, He hath sent me to heal the broken hearted, to preach deliverance to the captives, and recovering of sight to the blind, to set at liberty them that are bruised."

19) "To preach the acceptable year of The Lord."

The Lord did not come in September of 2012 because all the prophecys concerning Him were not fulfilled.

We must have faith in God; so we read on in the Bible to find in Matthew 24:48 "But and if that evil servant shall say in his heart, my Lord delayeth His coming".

Now in 2013, the chapter 13 talks about the coming of the antichrist, King Juan Carlos of Spain (see page 33).

The present Pope, Benedict The Sixteenth is retiring and we will have a newly elected Pope by the end of March 2013. This newly elected Pope will be the False prophet for the antichrist, King Juan Carlos of Spain. He eventually will be killed by the antichrist as described in Daniel 8:6 and 7.

The first year of the seven year Tribulation period has started at new years day 2013. 2013 or chapter 13 of the Book of Revelation describes the antichrist as receiving a wound in the head that is lethal; but the devil who is kicked out of heaven reincarnated him back to life. Rev: 13:3 "And I saw one of his heads as it were wounded to death, and his deadly wound was healed; and all the world wondered after the beast".

The opening of chapter 13 of Revelation; John talks about a beast rising out of the sea; having seven heads and ten horns. that is the antichrist, King Juan Carlos of Spain.

The seven heads that are described are his life long association with the catholic religion; he's a catholic. The ten horns that you see are the ten nations that form the original Roman empire; that he dominates after losing three of the then thirteen nations at the start of his acceptance as leader of The European Common Market.

The newly elected Pope will promote the antichrist and perform miracles in the sight of the beast. To deceive the world; saying to the world that they should worship the image of the first beast which had a lethal wound to the head and did live.

The Saint Patrick's Cathedral in New York City is equipped with three halographic projectors that will be used for the Antichrist prophet to use when he calls on fire to come down from heaven.

I don't know if that is the place were the fire from heaven will take place; but the cathedral is set up for it.

In chapter 17, the whore of Revelation is described having ten horns. (Rome is a member of the ten nation body; because the Vatican is it's own country). It sits on seven heads; (these are the seven mountains of Rome.)

The catholic church has changed the ten commandments, Get out of the catholic church. Believe in Jesus Christ as you Savior and Lord only, do not any substitute God to worship here on earth.

That's the weakness of the members of the catholic church; they always have had a priest or the POPE to be at their head; and they honor man. You cannot put your trust in a man for your salvation.

CHAPTER 9

"Introduction to the Book of Revelation"

The tribulation Hand-Book by Albert J. Lynch

The time you are in; is called The Tribulation Period. This period lasts seven years. The first 3 and a half years are called minor Tribulation; while the second half of the seven year period is called The Great Tribulation.

Our Lord Jesus Christ; who knows the future; had a witness to the events that are to happen in their respective years written down for posterity.

This list of events are in the chapters 12 thru 22 in the Book of Revelation.

Again I would have not found this out unless; I had written the Message.

In the message, we learned that Our Lord wanted to come earlier for His Church of Believers but delayed His coming. This delay was to fall in line with the third world war; between communist Russia and The United States over Isreal.

In the following pages; you will see how the years ahead have events that have been recorded by John The Apostle for your reading.

Note: John the Apostle was the only Apostle of Jesus Christ that died a natural death. His punishment for not being a Jew; but a Christian Believer was to be confined to the island of Pathmos until he died.

In the first Chapter: John describes The Seven that make up the time period; since He, Jesus Christ came on this earth.

All these Churches in Asia minor are in Greece.

Note: The Jews at the time of Christ had no word for gentile; you were either a Jew or a Greek. Greeks were also not Jews. They were non-believers of the Jewish Faith. They were foreigners to Judaism; And also not of the land of Isreal.

A great many of these people accepted Jesus Christ as their Lord and Savior; but also many would not accept Him.

These people that would not accept the Lord Jesus Christ as their Lord and Savior are in the Last Church of Laodicea, which you now reside.

But The Lord wishes that non be lost. Listen to what He says to The members of the Church Of Laodicea, The last Church, The Church of The Tribulation period. In Rev. 3:21.

"To him that overcometh will I grant to sit with me in my throne, even as I overcame, and am set down with my Father in His Throne." Thats the same reward as given to the other Churches who have been raised up at the Rapture of The Believers.

Description	Year		
A leap year. The acceptable Year of The Lord: as proven in the Publication of "The Message". The Book Of Revelation ties in chronological order Rev: 12:9 to the acceptable Year Of The Lord. The following chapters relate to the year; thru 22; or 2022, the last year, the start of eternity.	2012		The Seven Year Tribulation or The Seventh Week of Daniel
The year of the antichrist; King Juan Carlos of Spain, is shot in the head; and is reincarnated by the devil; who is kicked out of heaven at the same time as the believers in Jesus Christ are Ruptured up to heaven. The antichrist becomes the leader of the European common market. He kicks out three nations, to form the original Roman empire. New pope. Build New Jewish Temple. EZ. 40	2013	Minor Tribulation	
The New Pope becomes the antichrist Prophet. 144 thousand from the twelve tribes of Isreal; receive a seal of Salvation. The mark of the beast is started on the people of the earth that are left with the antichrist. Antichrist battles Russia and wins with God's help. Seven plaques from God the Father. Jews flee the antichrist to Petra. Warning about the Mark. 666 in the Right hand or Forehead.	2014		
The New Pope performs Evil Miracles; promoting the antichrist. Sores are put on men who have received the mark of the beast. Water turns to blood. The sun scorches the men who have taken the mark of the beast. Seven angels having the last seven plaques from Father God; Having the wrath of God for men that have taken the mark of the beast.	2015		
The Battle of Armageddon, where the Blood of those killed reaches up to the horse's bridle. The center of the Tribulation period; when the antichrist steps into the Holy of Holies in the new Ezekiel chapter 40 temple and says, He is God. A leap year.	2016		

Description	Year		
The Devil, Satan Kills the Pope, his prophet. The Great whore in Rome and the catholic church is hated by all nations. Rome is burned with fire.	2017	↑	
All the merchants and Kings of the earth shall mourn the passing of the the great whore, the catholic church. And in her was found the blood of prophets, and of saints, and all that were slain upon the Earth.	2018	Major Tribulation	
The final battle between Good and evil. The Lord Jesus Christ sits on a white horse with the sword of the word of God out of his mouth; and takes on all the all the nations that worshipped the beast; and wins. The beast and the false prophet, and those which worshipped the beast and took the mark of the beast were thrown into the lake of fire.	2019	↓	
Marriage supper of the Lamb; the Church of Believers in Jesus Christ as their savior and Lord live a thousand years on the earth with the Lord While the Devil, the antichrist, and the false prophet are in torment in the lake of fire for a thousand years. The last two feast days of the Law of Moses are celebrated this year. A leap year. Tribulation ends.	2020		The Seven Year Tribulation or The Seventh Week of Daniel
New Jerusalem comes down from heaven. A new earth with no oceans. To accommodate the amount of people who are saved from all the nations of the earth through time. The Believers of Jesus Christ, are treated to a thousand years of life on the new earth. Those who did not take the Mark.	2021		
The beginning of eternity, the believers in Jesus Christ are treated to a thousand years of life; in their earthly bodies. The tree of lifewith it's twelve fruits; and the leaves to heal the nations. No more time till a thousand years runs out; the the final judgement of all those who are not listed in the Lamb's Book of Life. No more time; just eternity.	2022	∞	

The End of Time is going to happen on July 7, 2013; with the Rapture of The Church of Christian Believers taken to Heaven by Jesus Christ.

According to the 13th Chapter of the Book of Revelation: The antichrist will show up to take over control of the ten nation entity in Europe called the Common Market. He will kick out three nations and the final membership will reflect the original membership of the Roman nations that Rome controlled in the time of The original Roman Empire.

You must be aware of the antichrist is a Roman, and also a Spanish King Juan Carlos. He is as old as I am; 74 years of age. Time is running out for him and me also. See the enclosed chart on 666.

As you can see from the chart; he has been given the title of "King of Jerusalem" by the Pope that corrinated him king in 1974. This event is described in Revelation chapter 13:13

13:13 "And He doeth great wonders, so that he maketh fire come down from heaven on the earth in the sight of men."

For your information three halographic projectors are set up in Saint Patrick's Cathedral in New York City; This where I believe it will take place. Of course I don't know if this is the pope at this present time of February 19th 2013 that will do the honors of bringing Fire down from Heaven; or another who will succeed this present one.

Also in Chapter 13:3 The antichrist receives a sword in the head and physically dies; but the devil who is kicked out of second Heaven incarnates King Juan Carlos's Body and raises him up to life.

This can be seen in the 666 chart; as the full name of Juan Carlos is not used in the computation of 666. This is because he is not all there.

The people who takes the mark of the beast are forced to worship an image of the beast. That is Rev. 13:15.

The Church of Believers is taken off the Earth before the Devil comes down from second Heaven to occupy the body of king Juan Carlos. This is confirmed in Rev; 12:9; as The Christian Believers are taken up in The Rapture of The Church of Believers in Jesus Christ The devil is kicked out of Heaven; so that we, The Believers will not have any contact with the Antichrist or his prophet.

Our God has laid out the order of events concerning the believers in His Acceptable year of the Lord. Our God is the giver of all good things. We are brought into this year of the heathen 2013 the evil that come from that little Russian, the dictator of Russia, who will set the end of the world in motion in the Peace and second peace with Isreal. This is described in Ezekiel 38 and 39 chapters where the third world war takes place between The United States and communist Russia over the state or should I say the nation of Isreal. God thru the antichrist defeats Russia and their cohorts.

Although most of the world is destroyed. The United States is no longer a world power. That would my guess of the point of the Rapture of The Church of Believers.

Just prior to that event; the world and all it's creatures are preached to about the Gospel of Jesus Christ.

Some would say that 2013 is just another year; but in God's acceptable order of things; it is the year of the antichrist. Or the first full year of the seven year Tribulation period.

After the war between The U.S.A. and communist Russia; Isreal will rebuilt their temple on the Temple Mount. They will offer sacrifices in memorial to God. The New Temple is described for construction in Ezekiel Chapter 40. The obstruction of the dome of the Rock falls in the other court and possess no problem.

The Arch of the Covenant has already been seen by the Jews in a place called Solomns vault. It is in the Arab section of Rooms under the temple mount, The Arabs have made access to it impossible with the wall of concert.

The Tribe of Levi are training priest to restore the offerings with the Arch of the covenant in place, in the new Ezekiel Temple. The tribe of Levi were assigned by God, out of the twelve tribes to care for and move the arch of the covenant back in Genesis.

In Chapter 14 of the Book Of Revelation it describes 144,000 people who are given God's mark of Salvation. These are men who have not defiled themself with women; and are the first born of their familys. That appears in verse 4 of Revelation 14.

Don't forget that anyone who does not believe in Jesus Christ as their Lord and Savior; and was sent by The Father God to redeem the world; is going into the seven year tribulation period; where the devil in the person of the image of the antichrist will be their world leader. Any one who takes the mark of the beast will lose their Salvation of The Lord for sure; and have no chance of regaining what was lost from God. They will be condemned to the lake of fire.

Chapter 15 of the Book of Revelation starts off with the ones that did not take the mark of the beast taking their place in heaven.

Verse 5 shows seven angels coming out of The Temple of the Tabernacle of The Testimony in Heaven; having 7 plaques; and one of the four beasts gave the seven angels, seven vials of the wrath of God and no man could enter the Temple until the seven plaques of the seven angels were fulfilled.

Chapter 16 of The Book of Revelation pertains to the seven plaques of the seven angels. These seven plaques fall in line; one after the other; and they are devoted to the men that take the mark of the beast.

1) The first vial put a noisome and grievous sore upon the men

2) The second angel poured out his vial on the sea, and it became as Blood of a dead man; and ever living soul died in the sea.

3) The third angel poured out His vial on the rivers and they became as Blood.

4) The fourth angel poured out His vial on the sun; and power was given to Him to scorch men with fire.

5) The fifth angel poured out His vial on the seat of the beast and his kingdom was full of darkness, and they gnawed their tongues for pain.

6)   The sixth angel poured out His vial on the River Euphates, and the water was dryed up, that the way of the kings of the east might be prepared.

7)   The seventh angel poured out His vial in the air; and a great voice out of The Temple of Heaven, from the Thorne saying, it is done.

After that was a great earthquake such as was not since men were upon the earth. Citys were destroyed; and God remembered Babylon; and gave her a cup of wine of the Fierceness of His wrath.

And every island fled away, and the mountains were not found.

And there fell upon men a great hail out of Heaven, every stone about the weight of a talent (almost 58 pounds). and the men blasphemed God; because of the plaque of the hail.

In Chapter seventeen it describes the destruction of the the great whore, who sits on many waters. The beast that has seven heads and ten horns. The seven heads are the seven mountains that the city of Rome sits and the ten horns are the original members of the original Roman Empire; which She controls.

The ten horns are used by God to destroy Rome and burn her with fire; according to God's will.

In Chapter Eighteen, the members of the catholic church are urged to come out of the catholic and worship God without the use of priest; by going directly to God and not an intercessor.

Our God urging the people, which He calls My people not to be partakers of Hersins, and that ye receive not her plagues.

The light of a candle shall shine no more in thee, and the voice of the Bridegroom and of the Bride shall be heard no more in thee. For thy merchants were the great men of the earth; for by thy sorceries were all nations deceived. And in her was found the blood of the prophets, and of the saints, and of all that were slain upon the earth.

Chapter nineteen The people in heaven honor Our God for His promises that now have been fulfilled. We say Alleluia; Salvation, and glory and honor, and power, unto The Lord Our God.

The marriage supper of the Lamb takes place.

The final battle between Good and evil takes place with the Lord God, The Word of God, sitting on a white horse, with the sharp sword of The Word of God out of His mouth; going forth with all armies of Heaven on white horses to smite the nations; and He shall with a rod of iron; and He treadeth the winepress of the fierceness and wrath of almighty God.

King of Kings and Lord of Lords was on His vesture an on His thigh. An angel standing in the sun, and he cried with a loud voice, saying to all the fowls that fly in the midst of Heaven, come and gather yourselves together unto the supper of the great God. That ye eat the flesh of kings, and the flesh of captains, and the flesh of mighty men, and the flesh of horses and them that sit on them, and the flesh of all men, both free and bond, both small and great.

The beast was taken and with him the false prophet that wrought miracles before him, with which he deceived them that worshipped his image. These both were cast into the lake of fire burning with brimstone. And all that remained were slain by Him that sat on the white Horse with the sword of God that proceeded out of His mouth. And the fowls were filled with their flesh.

Chapter 20 of the Book of Revelation starts out with an angel comes down from Heaven with, having the key to the bottomless pit and a great chain in his hand. (Note: The angel had hands, and was a male; who said that angel were sexless.) And he laid hold on the dragon, that old serpent, which is the devil, and Satan, and bound a thousand years. And cast him into the bottomless pit, and shut him up, and set a seal upon him, that he should deceive the nations no more, till a thousand years should be fulfilled; and after that he must be loosed a little season.

Chapter 20:4 Then John who is the author The Book of Revelation thrones, and they that sat upon them, and judgement was given unto them: and I say the souls of them that were beheaded for the witness of Jesus, and for the Word of God, and which had not worshipped the beast, neither his image, neither had received his mark upon their foreheads, or in their hands; and they lived and reigned with Christ a thousand years. (The antichrist, has in his possession a laser pistol, complements of the United States of America, that will cut the head of a person off with no spilling of the blood; because it cauterizes the wound as it is cutting thru the neck of the person it is used on). But the rest of the dead lived not until the thousand years were finished. (These are the people who did not accept Jesus Christ during the Tribulation period of seven years and will stand judgement, at the final judgement.)

These people who will Judge; are the people of the first resurrection. These shall be priests of God and of Christ, and shall reign with him a thousand year. (Notice in the last sentence that part of the Trinity of God is exposed. "Priests of God and Christ shall reign with him. the signual person; there is two for one.")

And when a thousand years are expired; (This is in eternity.) Satan shall be loosed out of his prison. And shall go out to deceive the nations which are in the four corners of the earth. Gog and Magog, to gather them together to battle: the number of whom is as the sand of the sea.

And they went up on the breadth of the earth, and compassed the camp of the saints about, and the beloved city (Jerusalem) and fire came down from God out of Heaven, and devoured them.

And the devil that deceived them was cast into the lake of fire and brimstone, where the beast (human antichrist) and the false prophet (the catholic Pope of 2013) are, and shall be tormented day and night for ever and ever.

And I saw a great white throne, (This is the author of the Book of revelation, talking, Saint John the Apostle) and him that sat on it, from whose face the earth and heaven fled away; and there was found no place for them.

And I saw the dead, small and great stand before God; and the books were opened; and another Book was opened, which is the Book of life: the dead were Judged out of those things which were written in the Books, according to their works.

And the sea gave up the dead which were in it; and death and hell delivered up the dead which were in them. And they were judged every man according to their works.

And death and hell were cast into the lake of fire. This is the second death. And whosoever was not found in the Book of life was cast into the lake of fire.

Chapter 21 And I saw a new Heaven and a new earth: for the first Heaven and the first earth were passed away. And there was no more sea. (Room is needed for all the people who were in the Book of life.

And I, John saw the Holy city, New Jerusalem, coming down from God out of heaven, prepared as a Bride adorned for her husband.

And I heard a great voice out of heaven saying, behold the tabernacle of God is with men, and He will dwell with them, and they shall be His people, and God, Himself, shall be with them, and be there God.

And God shall wipe away all tears from their eyes, and there shall be no more death, neither sorrow, nor crying, neither shall there be any more pain: for the former things are passed away.

And He that sat upon the throne said, Behold, I make all things new. And He said unto me, write: for these words are true and faithful.

And He said unto me, it is done, I am the Alpha and Omega. The beginning and the end. I will give unto him that is athrist of the fountain of the water of life freely.

New Jerusalem descends out of heaven having:

1) Twelve gates, with twelve angels, and each gate having the name of one of the twelve tribes of Isreal on it. 3 gates to the north. 3 gates to the south. 3 gates to the east; and 3 gates to the west.

2) There is no temple there; because the Lord God Almighty and the Lamb are the temple of it.

3) the twelve gates were twelve perals

4) the Streets of the city were of pure gold, as it were transparent glass.

5) The city had no need of the sun, neither of the moon, to shine in it for the glory of God did lighten it, and the Lamb is the light thereof.

6) The nations of them which are saved shall walk in light of it. and the kings of the earth do bring their glory and honor into it.

7) the gates of it shall not be shut at all by day. for there is no night there.

8) Only the they that have their names written in the Lamb's Book of Life.

The New Jerusalem is the place on earth were God the Father and Jesus Christ will meet with the people that are coming there who have their names written in the Lamb's book of life.

Chapter 22 pertains to eternal life for the believer in eternity with the river of water proceeding out of the Throne of God and of the Lamb. The tree of life, which bare twelve manner of fruit; and yielded her fruit every month. And the leaves of the tree were for healing of the nations. Note. (There will be human beings or the believers that will need healing in their bodies).

And, Behold, I come quickly, and my reward is with me, to give every man according to his work shall be.

I am the Alpha and Omega, the beginning and the end, the first and the last.

The last chapter of the Bible; has all the work done earth in the process of Salvation for the inhabitants who were on the earth as we know it.

Also the chapter number 22 is the year that it is all over for the Good the Bad people who ever inhabited the earth. There is no future without the future that our God has made for us, the believers.

CHAPTER 10
"The Masonic Order is a Religion"

So you joined a Brotherhood, a brotherhood of The devil. Your membership in the Masonic Order requires you to have over you a Master Mason; one who will supposed watch over you to make sure you are doing good things; and you pay him dues once a month. Thats not being free. You are in bondage to you masonic order.

Here's what Jesus Christ and the Father say about this.

Matthew 23:8 "But be not called rabbi: for one is your Master, even Christ; and all ye are Brethern.: This means the only one Master is Jesus Christ, your God in Heaven. You cannot have two Masters.

I have to put the next verse in; Matthew 23:9 "And call no man your father upon the earth: for one is your Father, which is in Heaven".

That verse knocks out the catholic church as a religion; but I guess there are many Masons that are catholic also.

The antichrist, King Juan Carlos of Spain, is a high degree Mason. What do you think he is going to tell his lower degree brothers to do? Of course; take

THE TRIBULATION HAND-BOOK

the mark of the beast. 666 is being used on animals at this time for identification of ownership. Note a chart on the calculation of the antichrist is in the rear of this Book.

You if you are caught; will be offered to take the mark of the beast in your hand, atop the right hand or have the micro-chip injected by a needle to the middle of your forehead. If you would refuse to take the injection of the mark of the beast; you will be put to death. You must reject this mark of the beast, or identity injection. All who take the mark of the beast will forever loss their salvation and are condemned to live in hell for eternity with the devil, the antichrist; and the others who toke the mark of the beast. 666.

For a mason to be saved and be in the seven year Tribulation period is:

1) If you are a Jew and come out of Tribulation with out the mark of the beast; you will be saved; but you still have to accept Jesus Christ as your Savior, and Lord, God.

2) If you are the first born in your Family; you will be saved.

3) If you are a Jew and was sealed with God's seals described in Chapter 6 of the Book of Revelation.

4) You must not accept the mark of the beast; if you do, you will lose all possibility of Salvation forever. All men must die; no body gets out of this world alive; even the ones that are taken of the earth; have their physical bodies change changed to immortal beings as they meet their Maker in the air.

5) You must deny the Masonic Order. Albert Pike wrote a Masonic Hand-Book around the turn of the first of the twentyeth century; and in it, he said "The God of Masonary is the Devil". This appears on page 174.

Most of the members of the Masonic Order do not advance above the third degree. They are to busy making relationships with their fellow brothers. They never find out the truth.

As the Masonic Brothers advance themselves into the higher degrees; they can make their material requirements; made known to the angel of light. This is the Devil himself!

The Bible verse that clarifies this is: 2 Corinthians 11:14, "And no Marvel: for Satan, himself is transformed into an angel of light".

This angel, Satan has no light of his own; the light that is seen is form God on His Thrown in The First heaven; the light of God shines down to second Heaven where Jesus Christ is battling the devil over the sins of the saved members of the Church of Believers.

The devil is the great accuser. See chart on page 37.

Diagram of The night of the Rapture of Christian Believers

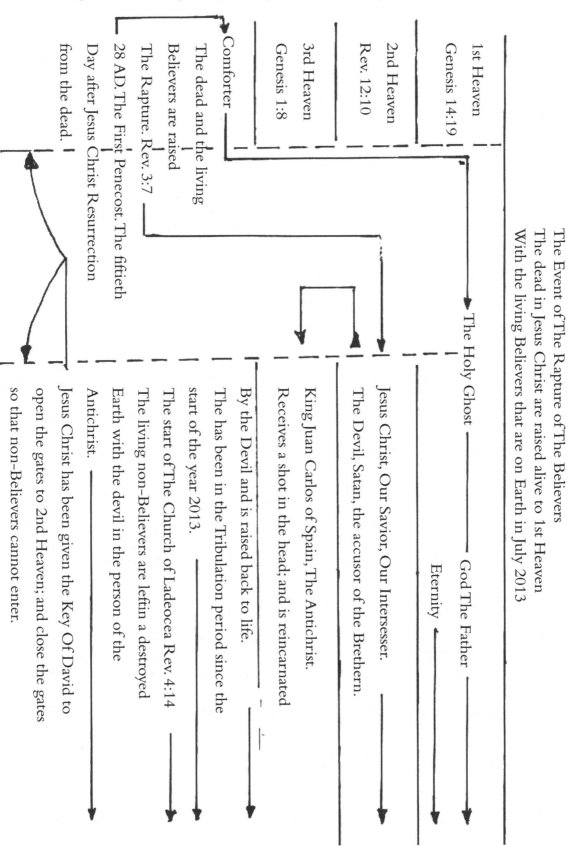

1st Heaven
Genesis 14:19

2nd Heaven
Rev. 12:10

3rd Heaven
Genesis 1:8

Comforter

The dead and the living
Believers are raised

The Rapture. Rev. 3:7

28 AD. The First Penecost. The fiftieth
Day after Jesus Christ Resurrection
from the dead.

The Holy Ghost ———

God The Father ———

Eternity

Jesus Christ, Our Savior, Our Intersesser.

The Devil, Satan, the accusor of the Brethern.

King Juan Carlos of Spain, The Antichrist.
Receives a shot in the head; and is reincarnated

By the Devil and is raised back to life.
The has been in the Tribulation period since the
start of the year 2013.

The start of The Church of Ladeocea Rev. 4:14

The living non-Believers are leftin a destroyed
Earth with the devil in the person of the
Antichrist.

Jesus Christ has been given the Key Of David to
open the gates to 2nd Heaven; and close the gates
so that non-Believers cannot enter.

The Event of The Rapture of The Believers
The dead in Jesus Christ are raised alive to 1st Heaven
With the living Believers that are on Earth in July 2013

Explanation of Page 51 for all you people that have never read the Bible.

The end of time is the end of time as we; the ones who live on this earth know it. It is accented with the destruction of the world as we have been living on. The fact is there will be a war between The United States and Russia; that will reduce the United States to less than a world leader; with the antichrist taking over as the leader of a one world government.

At the dame time as the world war 3 starts; our God and Lord will rescue His Christian Believers from the face of the earth and the leadership of the devil, Himself in the person of the antichrist. This all happens at the same moment in time.

Also The Holy Spirit is removed from the earth; so that the antichrist and devil can do there thing with the people that are left behind on the earth. The Holy Spirit is the third person of The Holy Trinity who protects the Christian Believers on earth before the end of time.

The future runs out for the devil and the antichrist in less than seven years; it also runs out for the people like you who have been left behind on the earth, the destroyed earth.

If you are one of these people; there is no future for you in taking the 666 mark and agreeing to the antichrist wishes. You must make a decision to what to live forever by not giving in to the devil and taking the mark of the beast.

CHAPTER 11

"Why is ther Tribulation Period?"

We do not live in a world; we created. No, we live in a world that God in Heaven created for us to live in. This is called third Heaven, as on the diagram on page 14,

God, The Father, who created you and me wants to see that we need him. We are free to accept Him, as our Lord and Savior; or not accept Him and believe the lies of the devil.

Now the Devil was put here on earth before we came (man). He knows he is condemned to hell for eternity; but his Judgement has not yet come up yet.

So he, the devil, and his demons; these are fellow fallen angels who also are condemned with the Devil, Satan. This group of condemned spirits are wandering around the earth; looking for others to ruin the hope of salvation. The old saying misery loves company".

Tribulation is here to test the fallen inhabitants of the earth; to see what they will do; to save themselves. God, wishes that no one be lost.

He has great rewards for the people who can make it out of this seven year period and enter Heaven; where the previously raptured people are waiting for The tribulation period to be over.

I pray that every one who reads the Bible and reads these words to help; will find the conviction in their heart to do what is the right thing to do. Show the THE ANTICHRIST HAS NO POWER OVER YOU; MUST MAKE YOUR OWN DECISION WHETHER OR NOT YOU WILL FOLLOW HIM TO DESTRUCTION; OR NOT FOLLOW.

Note: On the next page is a hand-out I gave out by personally putting on cars that were in Church parking lots before September 17, 2012. Again I believe we were given an additional three months time. Also to have some people that were setting on a fence to get off on the right side. Also the computation of the 666 as it relates to the antichrist.

I have been handing out these 666 papers since 1987. He was known before that. In 1975 there was a Doctor Charles Taylor who appeared on Chicago Television on a Sunday at 4:00 P.M. with his show called "Today in Bible Prophecy". This man knew who the antichrist would be in the person of the newly crowned King of Spain.

I met him once and showed him what is on the next page and he was impressed. The idea of submitting the alphabet to the number 6 in progression is not my idea; but the notes are mine. I thank whoever made up the code to show who is the antichrist.

None on this earth could complete these qualifications except him.

CHAPTER 12

"Calculation of the Person of the antichrist who is King Juan Carlos"

King Juan Carlos is also a high degree mason

The Catholic Church has changed the Ten Commandments

Explains Bible Verse Revelation 13:8   (original 9-18-1987)

What Man's name adds up to 666. Who is the Antichrist?

Substitute a numerical value for our alphabet to the base 6.

Add 6 to every total of the previous letter.

A=6	B=12	C=18	D=24	E=30	F=36	G=42
H=48	I=54	J=60	K=66	L=72	M=78	N=84
O=90	P=96	Q=102	R=106	S=114	T=120	U=126
V=132	W=138	X=144	Y=150	Z=156		

Words or Phrases that add up to 666.

Computer.......................666

Mark of the* Beast............666

Lucifer & Hell.................666

Lucifer & Hades...............666

Devil & Sheol..................666

People & Sin....................666

From Spain.....................666

Catholic Dogma...............666

Don J. Carlos..................666

All these words or phrases using this method of calculation add up to 666. The comparative examples confirm this method of computation.

The present King of Spain.

Bible Prophecy that this man Fulfills:

1) (King Juan Carlos) His full name is not used in the calculation. He is killed by a head wound and raised back up by the incarnation of the Devil. Revelation 13:3

2) "and the people of the prince to come shall destroy the city and the Sanctuary". Daniel 9:26—He was born in Italy to parents that were Ambassadors To Italy from Spain. Therefore he is a Italian, Roman. Jewish Temple was ruined in 70 AD.

3) Spain became the eleventh nation to join the Common Market in the year 1-1-1986. This fulfills Daniel 7:8

4) There are thirteen nations in the Common Market now in 1996. This is the total number of members before he takes over; and kicks out three to make ten nations. The same nations will be the original

member nations that made up the Roman Empire. This will fulfill Daniel 7:20.

5) He shall stop the daily sacrifice in the new Jewish Temple an commit the Abomination of Desolation when he goes in the Jewish Temple and proclaims himself God. Daniel 8:13.

Chapter 13

"The End of Time"

I was looking up the word end in my concordance and came across about twenty entries in the Bible, and as I looked over the first ten; I came across Ezekiel chapter 7; which I think deals with the subject at hand.

Ezekiel, Chapter 7;

"Moreover the word of The Lord came unto me, saying also thou son of man, thus saith the Lord God unto the land of Israel; and end is come upon the four corners of the land. Now is the end come upon thee, and will judge thee according to thy ways, and will recompense upon thee all thine abominations. And mine eye shall not spare thee, neither will I have pity; but I will recompense thy ways upon thee and thine abominations shall be in the midst of thee; and ye shall know that I am The Lord.

Thus saith the Lord God; an evil, an only evil, behold is come. An end is come, the end is come; it watcheth for thee, behold, it is come.

The morning is come unto thee, othou that dwellest in the land. The time is come, the day of trouble is near, and not the sounding again of the mountains.

Now will I shortly pour out my fury upon thee, and accomplish mine anger upon thee and I will judge thee according to thy ways, and will recompense thee for all thine abominations.

And mine eye shall not spare, neither will I have pity, I will recompense thee according to thy ways and thine abominations that are in the midst of thee, and ye shall know that I am The Lord that smiteth.

Behold the Day, behold, it is come: the morning has gone forth the rod hath blossomed, pride hath budded.

Note: The author can see from this passage that after authoring "The Message" where a specific date was referred too. That I believe the end of time will occur after the Fourth of July 2013. Probably anywhere from the 7th to the tenth of July 2013.

Our President Obama has been told by Vadmire Putin of Russia; that any aid to the Syrian rebels would result in an invite to a world war. Obama has given small arms to the rebels; at this time He is afraid that His help might fall into the wrong hands; so he is proceeding with caution.

The time of this writing is the 23rd of June 2013.

This is put here for you readers to see that our warns the believers ahead of time if He is going to do something.

It is nice to know that He changed His mind from the 16-17 of September 2012 till now. He gave us extra time, His coming will fall into the place of the war between Russia and the United States. The Worlds War Three.

If you can get a 1611 King James Bible; before the antichrist has them all collected and burned. Read Ezekiel Chapter 7 for yourself.

There is only one way out of your situation; and that is to deny any and all of what the antichrist wants you to believe.

You commit your life to the Savior of the World Jesus Christ.

BIBLIOGRAPHY

Holy Bible (In large print).

Gaint print

Nelson

Regency 88icbg

Copyright 2003 By Thomas Nelson Inc.

All rights reserved

2829303131-0807060504

Strong's Concordance of the Bible.

A popular Edition of exhaustive Concordance.

Copyright 1980 By Thomas Nelson Publishers.

"The Message" By Albert J. Lynch in 8½ x11

Copyright 2012 Albert J. Lynch

Trafford Publishing Inc.

ISBN 978-1-4669-4705-4